DON'T EXPLAIN

The Felix Pollak Prize in Poetry
The University of Wisconsin Press Poetry Series
Ronald Wallace, General Editor

Now We're Getting Somewhere · David Clewell
Henry Taylor, Judge, 1994

The Legend of Light · Bob Hicok
Carolyn Kizer, Judge, 1995

Fragments in Us: Recent and Earlier Poems · Dennis Trudell
Philip Levine, Judge, 1996

Don't Explain · Betsy Sholl
Rita Dove, Judge, 1997

DON'T EXPLAIN
Betsy Sholl

The University of Wisconsin Press

To Sandy,
I think of your
deco passionate
luminous poems
with great fondness
and admiration.
Your spirited
quiet passion,
deep warmth &
courage are
very special.
Love,
Betsy
Montpelier,
1999

The University of Wisconsin Press
2537 Daniels Street
Madison, Wisconsin 53718

3 Henrietta Street
London WC2E 8LU, England

1   3   5   4   2

Printed in the United States of America

Library of Congress Cataloging-in-Publication Data
Sholl, Betsy.
Don't explain / Betsy Sholl.
82 pp.   cm. — (Felix Pollak prize in poetry)
ISBN 0-299-15720-2 (cloth: alk. paper).
ISBN 0-299-15724-5 (pbk.: alk. paper)
1. Suffering—Poetry.   I. Title.   II. Series.
PS3569.H574D66 1997
811'.54—dc21   97-10796

Do you not see how necessary a World of Pains and troubles is to school an Intelligence and make it a soul?

—John Keats

Contents

Acknowledgments

Grateful acknowledgment is made to the editors of the
following publications where these poems first appeared:

The Alembic: "Blues Is My Companion,"
"Fine Arts," "Halfway," "Undersong"

The Beloit Poetry Journal: "Babysitting to Thelonious Monk,"
"Different Porches," "Four Crows at Dusk," "Sparrows"

Cafe Review: "Style" (under the title "The Aisle")

Cimarron Review: "Autobiography in Third Person," "Loose Keys"

Crab Orchard Review: "Chances"

Field: "Behind the Saint-Lazare Station," "Monkey House," "Mysterioso,"
"Test Patterns," "The Stream," "The Tiny Gate," "Redbud," "Valentines"

5AM: "Hood," "To the Dregs"

Indiana Review: "Don't Explain"

Missouri Review: "A Kind of Darkness," "Festival in the Park,"
"The Rim," "With You in the Darkness"

Nebraska Review: "The Past"

Thanks to the Maine Arts Commission
and the National Endowment for the Arts for
grants that made some of these poems possible.

I am deeply grateful to all the people who read this
manuscript or offered advice on individual poems,
including Susan Aizenberg, Ted Deppe, Nancy Eimers,
Barbara Hope, Tam Lin Neville, Bill Olsen, Pamela Stewart,
David Wojahn, and especially my companion, captive
audience, and fierce listener, Doug. Thank you to Rita
Dove for her generous reading of these poems.

I

BEHIND THE SAINT-LAZARE STATION

After the photograph by Henri Cartier-Bresson

Every day, seventh period, we'd look
at the photo over the teacher's desk,
till the word RAILOWSKY on the station wall
started a whole year of fake Polish,
perfected by a boy we called Joe
Needs-A-Whiskey. I can still see him posed
under the principal's glare: open shirt,
greased hair, a sullen Elvis. But in art class,
bent over his sketch pad, a softer Joe:
face slack, lost in concentration,

the way the photographer must have
forgotten himself behind that station
waiting for a perfect moment—caught,
as a man leaped off a prone ladder
into a rain-flooded lot, the water
doubling him in a sort of pas de deux.
And if the runner himself merely passed
through, his best moment occurring almost
without him? Well, it's an argument
I first heard from Joe, whistling Doo Wop

through his teeth, as he quick-sketched the page,
hardly looking at his hands. That's how
the photo was snapped, as if from inside,
photographer swept up in the man's run
across the ladder, the water repeating
his leap, dancers in the poster taking off
with it across the station wall. How'd you
do that? I'd sigh, after a swirling hand
and some off-key "Earth Angel" became
a wine bottle and pears on folds of cloth,

while my measured lines kept ending up
erasure smears tossed in the basket,
cartoon bottles I couldn't sweat into roundness.
That whole year I lingered in art class
long after the bell, not knowing why,
never expecting those moments to last—

3

Joe squinting over my crumpled sketches
for a shadow or line to like, taking
my stiff hand in his, scent of nicotine
and graphite, as we moved Ouija-like

across the page. English, math—anywhere
outside that room, you could follow the rules,
get somewhere. But there was Joe. There was this
photo saying, What's a straight line? What's time?
At the top of the ladder, we just kept
climbing, Joe riding my hand all over
the paper, across state lines. *Girlchik,*
he'd say, *we need a whiskey,* and he'd draw
till we were loose and giddy, as if we
had drunk whatever he put in my hand.

THE STREAM

Sign of the times, back then, how in one day
you'd be groin-shoved into a hydrant, half
faint, cop grinding a nightstick in your back,

then an hour later, aching in a stuffed chair
telling your first shrink how you felt dizzy
in that crowd, how shouting *peace, peace,*

you felt rage kick-start inside—a sweaty
bandannaed, avenging angel, itching
to gouge somebody's lawn. Years, and what's left

of that session is the shrink's bored expression,
me staring out the window at children splashing
in a fountain, that water's thin stream back

to firehoses in Birmingham, their fierce
spray like machine guns knocking the kids down
to writhe in mud, to slip and fall in black

and white, as shaky cameras panned the scene,
then focused on one scrawny girl just far
enough out of the stream to stay on her feet

when the water started. All arms and legs
she stood there doing the twist, her whole body
an exuberant stuck-out tongue. I wanted

to know the tune that girl carried in her mind
to replay after the cameras were packed
and gone, to keep the gawky dance aching

in her elbows and hips. I would have paid for that,
for the shrink to hum, "Twist and Shout." Years,
and what's left of that day are the black kids

who walked the crowd's edge, mocking our prissy
peacenik chants, jutting gloved fists in the air.
One pulled me out of the cop's grip, held me

a long time, crooning, "hush now, hush,"
his huge cloud of hair wrapped in a red bandanna.
And what I wouldn't tell the shrink was how

I loved being his baby, being held
in the stream of bodies till it carried us
someplace familiar and he let me go . . .

WITH YOU IN THE DARKNESS

For G. W.

Once again I find you,
celluloid, flammable, fallen from a book,
your unfocused stare swirling galaxies

between you and everything else in the room—
you and the sunlit plants, the baby lunging
in her walker toward the dog's ear—light-years

between you and your one photo as a boy
in front of a house you had forgotten was green.
It had 17 cats. You said your mother

was a whore—no forgetting that. And even then
your eyes were lost, unfocused—that look
how many men tried to knock out of you?

Your first skill—being hurt.
Then you showed me the second—posed
in a doorway, the various gestures of lure.

Somewhere in another photo you lean
on a trunk fallen across white rushing water
you once said symbolized death,

and it might as well be true, you look
so desolate, Uranian. How fitting then,
that it poured into the bullet hole you put

in your face, the uncloseable mouth. Nothing
but rain for days. Rain ran through ditches,
pooled around stones, softened the graveyard,

easing you into a dark stream my mind
has to resist. Against it, I write your name,
George, I remember the night you came down

those rickety stairs along the side of your house,
backless, rotting steps. My baby was sick.
You came out from the stench of cats

and drove, hunched over the wheel
of your green Volkswagen, forcing its thin beams
around switchbacks. Who knows what dark

gravities you had to resist to keep your gaze
fixed that night. Nurses swept my baby
through double doors, I was told to wait,

and there are no pictures of this—
your jittery refusal to leave, the torn mounds
of Styrofoam, ashtray of bent paperclips

you twisted into makeshift constellations
no one will ever see
if I leave these things where they belong.

TO THE DREGS

I saw my own children leaning
against the corner church. In streetlight
their eyes glittered, hard as the empty
pints and fifths they cast off—my own
smoldering kids lifting a bottle
of gasoline to their lips, flicking the lighter's
elongated flame, so their breath erupts.
Overnight, I was not a woman, not
even human, just two useless eyes.
What could I pour on a flaming child?
What could I do but drop like God's own grief?
Drink this cup, is what he said,
Stop and let it drench you——

THE RIM

Once my sister wrote me as her son stole
her car, typed out as it happened: engine rev,
squeal across three lawns, over a curb and gone,
as if more than wanting to stop him,

she wanted to be heard, that endless chore
left over from childhood, our purgatorial rim
where we work the street, griefs pinned
inside our coats like hot watches.

Such constant yakking—as if that could stop
silence from shuttling us straight down.
I'm reading about the years in Leningrad
they called *the Terror*—women waiting

outside prisons: first their bundles ransacked,
then the stamp's officialese, *whereabouts
unknown.* In Akhmatova's line, barely
a whisper broke, until the famous question,

"Can you describe this?" And her *Yes, I can*
made speech seem heroic. But how does it
help my sister to tell her: Once your boy
walked through yellow fields, collapsing

in elaborate comic deaths, riddled
by invisible bullets? We watched him
jump up, toss a stick, amble on through
autumn light, trees scattering their leaves

in great updrafts and eddies. Does it help
to remind her how even in the demon years,
he made those weekly bus treks
from the halfway house two hours across the city,

to sit with his grandmother and stroke her thin hair?
"Who are you," she'd whisper. He'd shake
his head and smile, eyes puffy with meds,
"Good question." There are so many:

When the pills ran down and the voices picked up,
who on the bus ride back would he accuse,
assassin or spy? What jittery child
would he eye, sawing shotguns in his mind—

until, in the hospital lockup, death came
by coatrack and belt. And now my sister,
like those other mothers, finds grief makes
the simplest chores impossible. It drives her

out of the store, groceries heaped on the counter,
manager in chase, until she turns on him
inconsolable eyes. No short cut through loss.
Bare trees worn down to winter-sheer nerve

stand along the road like women waiting
for word of a lost child, refusing to be exiled
from sorrow. "White winter," Akhmatova writes,
"on its knees, observes everything,"

and that may be all there is to explain
how she came to another rim, a shore
laced with ice, its air so luminous and thin,
day's end or world's hardly mattered.

Long past feeling cheated—numb, you could say,
but no—look how she describes this evening
light, rosy and resinous, falling on pines,
every petal of bark clear.

DIFFERENT PORCHES

I'm jiggling tips, so my fingers can smell
like money instead of the drunk who wouldn't
quit kissing on them as I sponged down the bar.
"I don't want to hear it," an old woman hollers

down the train platform, whips her head back
and forth, cries LA LA LA LA to a young man,
his hands abuzz, desperate to hush her.
Waiters were upending chairs, the moon

oozed down steamy windows. "Let's move it,"
my boss said to the creep, "you seat-belted
or what?" "What?" the young man tries to ask,
shaking his up-turned palms, tie loose, hair thick

as the mafia. Then softly he pleads, "Ma,"
"Come on," and the old woman blinks
like the air just snapped cables and plopped down
a son. Now, what can she do but vaguely push

at the buttons on his shirt, trying to soften
his terrible mentholated eyes? Nights like these,
who can be saved? Just being alive breaks a rule—
you talk, you feel, you trust something,

as the train rises above ground, arcs through
the factory district's gorgeous synthetic clouds.
Back home, I toss, my own thoughts mixed
with the gravelly play-by-play of a Celtics

rerun next door. I look out, on what should be
the real world, and a car clatters over trolley tracks,
two men step from an unlit doorway,
checking their flies. On triple-decker porches

up and down the block, work clothes freeze-dry
in triplicate, names scrolled in oval patches—
Sonny, Lenny, Bill. They can't sleep either.
That's why our windows all flash the same score,

why we step out between stiffening pant legs
to gaze at the night's neon cardiogram,
and find this moon sailing through clouds,
like an old woman unhinged, cut loose

from her three-piece son. Different porches,
but it's the same long sigh. Somebody smells
smoke, somebody feels a cable snap and clicks
on the light. Me, I hear a dream preacher cry,

"Open your Bible to Matthew 29."

LOOSE KEYS

Sometimes fumbling among the loose keys
in the bottom of my purse, I wonder
about the locks they once fit, those
tumblers and latches long ago shipped
to another city or melted down in vats,
while the doors that held them, the houses
behind the doors slowly fall in status—

so when the radio host dubs his caller
"the dinosaur," like some prehistoric loser
who should have plugged into his advice—
"world's changing fast, my friend, and you're
lugging a history of steel-plated doors
around your thick maladaptable neck"—
I can't shut him off.

If it still exists, I could unlock
the office I once shared with the founder
of SDS, whom I never saw, just
his chalkboard scrawls like dinosaur tracks,
elaborate time lines chronicling
the rise of the military industrial
complex, that catastrophic climate shift.

I could unlock four houses, two churches
and one architectural firm—if they
aren't just some "peculiar wrinkle in
entertainment history," to quote
Tiny Tim now telling the radio host
how it crushes the pride to play
birthdays and bar mitzvahs.

Oh, the sour color, the hideous sound
of big stupid things dying clueless—
sound of Godzilla on continuous replay,
or AM radio rushing over
crackly PAs in sweatshops across
America, not to mention
the signal gone to screech in this tunnel's

commuter jam where all our anxious
pride revs and brakes, roaring *achieve,
achieve:* souped-up version of childhood's
elaborate prayers, those magic potions
of words we'd repeat each night to keep
our little worlds uncrushed another day.
I'd like to phone that know-it-all deejay,

and ask how we got so full of ourselves,
what it would take for something to reach down
through the heating grates, into the switch box
of our brains and shut off this incessant
furnace-rumble of Self, this grumbling,
expanding, sputtering star that pulses
into the cosmos its static-y blitz.

O dear monsters of childhood,
what went on in your small heads,
in your oversized everything else,
when you discovered you didn't make
survival's final cut? Dear lost creatures,
banging and slamming while the house
tumbled down around you, shrieking

and swinging your bewildered heads—
here and there a footprint, a knob of bone
give us a glimpse into how some other
species will piece together theories on us:
demise by meteor or ice, by clumsy
blustering, demise by wanting too much,
or not wanting anything nearly enough.

UNDERSONG

As if it's that easy—just breathe in, breathe out,
lips all floaty, hands relaxed. But I'm flashing
back to a halfway house fund-raiser
in the after-hours aquarium where it wasn't
dark enough for the phosphorescent fish.

Halfway to black-out, somebody wearing my clothes,
downed flute after plastic flute of champagne,
and still wasn't glowing, so why should the fish?
Maybe they were trying though, whatever it takes
to get lit, pushing, squeezing, moving their lips—

gestures I remember from my grade school
stammer, trying to squeeze out an *f* or *s*.
Years ago, and here we are again, fast-forward
past the aquarium to this class on prayer,
still trying to navigate between withhold

and release, numb out and feel. I close my eyes
and flashy little Day-Glo speed freaks hustle
the walls of their tank, angel and devil fish.
Who would have thought prayer could look
like a bad trip? But memory has this way

of plastering the eye with decals, so the only
holiness I picture is hurricane wind, one of those
revved up storms that blew through our town
like bikers, emptying boardwalk bars, swilling
the bay through streets, splintering docks

into Popsicle sticks. And now we're asked
to say what ballast we're willing to chuck,
what crates of rage, oil drums of guilt, like it's
just an easy tumble backwards over the side,
not to worry, a friendly dissolution:

just relax those white knuckles, think: huge
fluency, voices effervescing as they fall.
Think: shimmy and sway of creatures already

16

arrived where they always wanted to be,
see-through gelatinous flowers, bright

synchronicities of fish—until in spite
of myself, an extravagance of whale song
erupts in my mind, humpbacked hallelujahs,
beluga and sperm song, killer and blue
praising what they pass through, what passes

through them: such infinitesimal phantasms,
tiniest ash of plankton glitter, phonemes
relieved of grammar, bodies of weight,
effortless sway of water and tide shift,
and world without rift. Amen.

STYLE

Black slacks and a red blazer in public school—
every morning in those halls, you'd slide the last
few feet to your locker, while a chorus of guys

waved limp wrists, or lisped—hands on hips—
Good Morning, Wilhelmina. Sometimes a jock
would stick out his chinoed leg, and you'd

stumble, Billy, though I never saw you fall.
I can close my eyes and still hear your voice
telling me how to dress up style's basic black,

or cursing your sister's preening thug of a boyfriend.
Then your father's heavy steps, dark mood coming in
from closing the bar, and the phone's click.

Next morning, dark glasses, coffee on your breath—
for years I thought that was the smell of bruises.
Nights we parked at the river, your spidery hands

running a strand of my hair across your mouth—
maybe I liked it that way, your chapped lips
on my forehead never growing urgent.

I still remember our visit to that couple
from your old school—teenagers with two babies,
four parents giving them a week at the shore

for passing their GEDs. What a scene—
the fluttering clump of them, loaded with umbrellas,
coolers, thick Jersey accents, fussing lotion

onto each other's backs. *Wouldn't you give anything,*
you asked later, *for that?* We were standing
on my front lawn, my mother called from a window

that it looked cheap—you peeling big patches of skin
off my back. I remember your lashes
unnaturally black, and you didn't promise to call—

so now what lingers is your glide down that hall,
refusal to stiffen your wrists, your incredibly light kiss
on the raw new under-layer of my skin,

saying good-bye for the rest of our lives. Your life,
Billy, I can't imagine now, though I know it isn't cheap.
Everything you did was dark with style—

your sister's wedding, the way you rushed in
after the organ had begun, took her supermarket daisies,
giving her instead one long-stemmed black rose,

and even as your father yanked her to the aisle,
you were thumbing mascara from her bruised cheek,
whispering, *Sweetheart, don't, don't.*

MYSTERIOSO

If you jiggle the book of Russian icons
the cloth on God's knees shimmers like the suit
Thelonious Monk wears in *Straight No Chaser*—
sharkskin shifting as he leans into the keys
picking up shadow and light—almost grooved

like those old Cracker Jacks cards giving us
two scenes we could jiggle back and forth:
a boy's smile flipping into a scowl, the world
notched and mutable—or in another light
a child might assume whatever was playing

on a person's face, there was an opposite
lurking behind. And that's just how it is,
my friend would say, we're both sides of the coin,
head and tail pressed, the way in the movie,
Monk rasps a few unintelligible words,

then sits down to his bright clear riffs, their jab
and dodge against the dark—without which,
my friend insists, what's light? It's how
the mystics argue too: the soul just a rumor,
expensive perfume sealed in a flask,

until it's broken. This same friend once felt
her life wasn't worth two bits. She downed
a bottle of pills, then walked, hoping to drop
unknown, no wallet, just a stiff in the morgue.
But God must have had different plans—

otherwise, she can't explain how the spare change
in her pocket, embossed head on a coin
under her thumb, made her feel her daughter's
real face, swollen by grief. It got her to a cop.
Doctors emptied her out—years of loathing,

finally gone. And the world came back
pure gift. She told me this when I was stuck
in a hard-luck story of my own, same side
coming up no matter how I flipped: loss
still loss, heartbreak still hoarding itself,

playing its rot-gut tunes no matter what
buttons I pushed. Which is why I love Monk,
who makes of the past such variations
in the confession booth of my car,
it's as if a tune's not a tune until it's stretched

more ways than you'd think it could go
without snapping. And when he snaps it,
what can you do but say *yes* to all that
discord and delay, those runs and aversions
you had to be hurt into hearing?

CHANCES

Behind the car peeling out with my daughter,
the boy's a cartoon of running, arms pumping,
legs high. I can't help thinking *thief*, like the kid
I saw in New York once, coming out of a store,
clutching something under his coat. *Hey,*

my friend called, *drop it*, and he did—boom box
splitting apart on the sidewalk as he took off.
Now the car rounds the corner again, honks
to make this boy look up from his gasping
and climb in. *Hey, Baby*, my daughter calls,

half her body stuck out the window—
sixteen, off for a night at the boardwalk,
where everyone's part cheat, trying to con
the numbers and iffy rides, toss darts
against the odds neon flashes through slats

onto the dark water brooding below.
The tide's contained now, but come a storm,
it'll swell and batter the pilings, tumble a girl
like dice on a wheel. I have flashbacks—
waves heavy with sand, crashing down so I can't

get my head out. You'd think I dropped as far
as Pip, the cabin boy in *Moby Dick*,
plummeting through briny sub-basements
where the world's weight is stored, tumbling,
bottomless, nothing to stand on. What could he do

after that, but stare, bug-eyed, addressing himself
in third person like the people on park benches
ducking mortar from an old war, or nodding
to a conversation started years ago?
On the pier where the kids wander from ride

to ride, my daughter will turn the barkers' heads
with her yellow hair, as she goes to test
night's loud music and chintzy lights, shrieks

scattered over the water from frenzied carousels.
Easy enough to shrug, *Why not*—this edge,

huge ocean rolling in, against which
we pitch our ridiculous coins. Why not
plunge through the mazes and wheels
of those rigged games, taking another
and another chance, trying for some

perfect shot to realign our lives?
But that's not how it felt the night my child's
blood pressure dropped, and her life flickered
so far from jackpot she didn't want to wake up.
Too late for a stomach pump, they ran IVs

and I don't ever want to see again
that shade of pale and fear. Later, she flushed
what was left of those pills. We held each other
watching them swirl, and if I can say this now,
it's because sometimes the waves spit us back up—

Delivered from the deep, Jonah says.
And that's how the houses look near the boardwalk,
on their green weedy stilts, one with a wall
like the slat backing of an old radio
showing the circuitry inside, wires and tubes

where current flows. Does every kid half-live
in the radio, receiver tuned to those jacked-up
voices of longing and rage? I can still hear
Cousin Brucey advertising Palisades
Amusement Park, its tattooed barkers

with their nicotine kisses calling *Baby,*
Baby, as if we went there to lose our names,
whispering, *any life but mine.* Poor Pip.
The harpooners stood up to aim, and without
thinking he jumped, then found to his surprise

there isn't another life. Refuse our own,
and we're left to drift between stations,
on oceans of static. Imagine—the boats
take off, the huge water expands its bad trip
around you. Terror in the depth, terror

in the width. *Heartless immensity, my God!*
Melville writes—as if vastness dissolves us.
To keep himself solid, Jonah quoted psalms
in the belly. When the dark rose up like waves
slamming my daughter, she says she drifted

in and out, repeating all night, *don't die.*
It takes my breath away—to think how the pills
we saw spin down the drain could have swallowed
that voice, swept it out so far she'd never get back.
It's happened enough. You can see them

on the boardwalk, drifters caught in the undertow.
They mutter to figments of themselves, ask
for spare change or a light, hoping to strike up
with a girl young enough to misread the signs,
and I can't help being relieved when my daughter

comes in, telling how a barker slowed down
the wheel so she could bring home this glass vase,
the color of water, air bubbles trapped inside
like breath rising from a diver, its value
in all the chances she took to get it.

II

BLUES IS MY COMPANION

I

On the radio, Eddie Kirkland, bluesman, talking
with a deejay about the road—long string
of one-nighters, then Sunday mornings driving

through small towns, folks gathering for church . . .
Once he pulled off the road with his guitar,
started strumming, and it seemed a whole woods

full of birds, who'd been making the craziest racket
hushed right up. Half the morning he tested it—
man sing, bird hush, man still, bird squawk like mad.

Says he could live off that a long time. *Eddie,*
Eddie Kirkland, ladies and gentlemen—the deejay
starts a tape, and it's blues you can dance to.

You have to put down your paring knife and move.
Dinner can wait. You have to tear out time
and place, tape it to the wall, newsprint

photo of his face, tilted back in light, all sweat
and gleam. Forget black & white, forget history
with its great divides, its SWAT team of assumptions

swarming in. Here's mystery, ladies and gentlemen.
Plays an upbeat blues, town after no-name town.
Says he just lets the music bubble and smoke,

till all those tired folk can't help but dance.
Mississippi to Chicago—carried him
sixty years, in and out of trouble, in and out

of war, rotgut, Jim Crow, those steel-string hungry,
those battered, hocked, rebought—those backroom
to spotlight, sweet, get-up Child, blues.

II

For years I wouldn't turn on the radio,
wouldn't let any kind of music get
to me, after growing up with my sister

who breathed it, drank it like soda—music,
instead of movies, guys, the phone, whatever
the rest of us were using for flotation.

I hated the way we'd be talking, I'd
be getting to the juicy part, then
suddenly she'd tilt her head so I knew

what was coming: *Shhh, shhh,* and whatever
I was whispering (sobbing)—"the teacher said
she'd flunk me," "then he put his hand on my—"

was nothing. What was the something she heard
instead? I couldn't tell, I'd be so backed up
with the choked off sentence, the words like phlegm.

(Can you just swallow them? Don't they have to
go somewhere?) When I caught my breath, blinked,
there she'd be raising and lowering the trap

door to the attic, unfolding its scratchy creak
and spring, elongating then snapping the pitch.
Or she'd be off to the keyboard, sounding

one note, a handful maybe, as if she'd caught
only a small riff of it herself, just a breath
of this half-heard thing. I hated the way

it was always more important than
my story, her great pneumatic hush,
that cathedral door shutting in my face.

III

But there's a moment in a B.B. King song
the guitar holds a note, then the sax comes in,
same pitch, and keeps going higher

as the guitar falls away. "Sweet sixteen,
and you wouldn't do nothing for me."
Every time it comes round on the tape,

say I'm jogging, something hushes inside,
gets clarified—something I hadn't known
was jumbled. Low-down words, it's true,

but then music takes over, lament
pushing out of lechery into loss
so palpable it fills the body, the song

plugged into a communal dirge—like birds
lifted out of territory and hunger,
given rest from their frenzy. *Frenzy?*

Would they suddenly see it that way?
Dull ordinary brown birds in the shade,
until the music flushes them into

the most amazing sun-struck indigo.
"When I lost my baby I found the blues
instead." You can live off that a long time

if you have to, the way on live recordings
an old singer will sometimes clear his throat
so you can feel the knot in yours,

feel it pass through—a pushed-down,
kind of stepped-on thing at the back of the song.

FESTIVAL IN THE PARK

Tough times and lots to lose—the singer croons
a low-down blues, and the sax almost sears the air.
Behind the bandstand, through trees, the sky's a yellow
rippling light, no smoke. Must be sunset's fire
that leaves things uncharred, not the hot smelting flames
of the steelyards, I still remember from the night
we stood on a bridge, lovers above those red hot ovens,

feeling spared. We were young, not seeing how it took
the whole sweating nightshift of steel workers bending
at open furnace doors to keep us up there—though
surely inside we felt the heat, some free-floating
shame, the way we chain-smoked and chattered,
those flimsy facades. Not fire, but an accident
that forced my teeth up into my jaw finally

injured my face enough, so a night nurse, sick of
the moans, held up a mirror, hoping to shock me
silent, with my own lips curled back, eyes blackened,
mouth torn. She didn't know I'd always feared
a monster inside, striking matches on my cheekbones,
trying to burn her way out, screaming *love me,*
love me, till everyone ran. Now on the stage

the singer howls like he's known a monster or two,
and the sax finds a way to hold those flames
in its brass bowl, let them out a little at a time.
It must be carnival lights through the trees,
though my eyes want it to be celestial
acetylene, heat with its rage dissolved,
as I know can happen, because once we had a house

restored after it caught the blaze from next door.
What I remember of that night, draped in blankets,
standing among rough engines, radio squawks,
sound of flames rushing our roof and steps—is how
in the fire's fierce judgment I just let go
pages and curtains of our life, old records, photos,
letters stacked in the closet. *Take them,* I hissed,

tired of holding back loss, almost excited
to see the roar—the same thrill which on those hospital
nights became my odd consolation, moving that
small mirror across my swollen cheeks and eyes. Now
at the foot of the stage, a heavy woman dances
alone, jiggling flesh, shooting arms in stiff thrusts,
while the singer growls—"you can do it, girl,"

as if he means, convert that weight into motion,
which is, I think, the power of flames. And maybe
I knew the moment I saw myself smug on the bridge
above those molten steelworks, I'd have to go down,
ring by ring, till some kind of heat blasted me into
a dazed shadowy thing. A little fire here—
could that spare us later, so when the light finally does

become liquid and pours over us, we won't be
all chaff and dross, turning away from its brightness?
Of course we see only dimly now, in a roulette flash,
or the ball-toss game where a young lover tries to win
for his gaunt-faced girl an oversized panda, till he's spent
all he has, and has to turn out empty pockets to her.
She slips bare arms around him, turning for a kiss,

and they stand, like us, among semis idling,
roadies pushing speakers up a van ramp, carnies
calling last chance for their tilting, whirling machines—
as if there isn't much time to let whatever can,
shake us down to the music's longing, to our own
unmasked faces, the singer's final rasp of "Mercy,
mercy," that still lingers as we drift away.

TEST PATTERNS

Someone on the street smiles in your direction
and you're not sure, but beam it back. Of course,
the gorgeous guy is really greeting the gorgeous
woman behind you, and now you're some kind of alien
from a hot red-faced planet, wishing for quick
transport to another erroneous zone, another warm
body you might attach to, to keep from swirling
into dissolution, another language to confess
your puny sorrows in before this broadcast day concludes
and sleep unplugs you. Perhaps you would like to see
those photographs of outer space, its hot galactic swirls
ignoring gravity, as if motion is all that matters
and everything comes down to it. Before that happens,
take a moment to recall light pricks through the steamy
windows of a parked car, say a boy whispering blunt
directions—*come, go, down, up*—you trying to talk stars
with him, why you feel like a cinder somebody's about to
scrape off a boot tread. "Shut up," he probably said,
smothering you with soggy lips. And it's not that
you wanted your initials projected onto the moon,
you just wanted that jerk to listen, wanted your breath
inducted into the atmosphere, rising—OK, thinning
to a molecule, just not fading out completely.
Don't forget that little kid holding up his hand
to halt Boston's rush hour. Standing on the corner,
he made his voice fatherish as he could, and you wanted
to stop for him, wanted him to believe in that hand,
those wishes, but it would have caused a five-car wipeout.
You had to go on, among the multitude teaching him
wishes are impotent, the world's full of ironically smiling
grills, among which he's a pathetic squint. That's why
you don't spend more clear nights on your back,
on the picnic table, swatting mosquitoes, admiring
the starry traffic jammed overhead. Though probably
the kid goes home, drinks a lot of milk, years pass,
he gets his license, and it's a good thing he doesn't
think he's king of the road, doesn't wrap his hand
across a girl's mouth, whispering she's beautiful like that.
Maybe he'll even talk to her, like the man
beside you now, chuckling as he falls asleep, who leaned

in a doorway once, stroking a cat so fondly it seemed
like a revelation: The world is created by touch,
Touch is good. *So what's the big deal?*
you heard a voice mutter inside, throaty, celestial.
Now, your thoughts drift into test patterns, big blobs
the shape of your head, or your shadow on the wall
this morning, when the light tried to pass through
and couldn't, so landed on you instead. Remember
how you closed your eyes and felt pure scintillation
backed up on your face—though it slipped through
the sieve of language, though nothing could calibrate
the force of that touch hitting the atmosphere,
busting into a jillion pieces at once.

THE PAST

I love hanging out laundry, bright linens,
billowy tables of air, and how when the pins slip,
wind like a mad lover tumbles a sheet
up gusty ladders, over treetops and roofs.

Birds flitting from branch to branch,
bright leaves, smoke from the neighbor's roof—
everything rises. Why should smoke hesitate
on the chimney's edge? Why should it

stiffen and fear sheet-fall, dog-snap, rag-rot,
the fire roaring below? In the book of Acts
our mother read to us, there's a chapter
where if you circled the words *rise, stand, get up,*

those whisper-thin pages would be full of eyes.
And if those words did what they said, there'd be holes
to see through, like stepping into brightness,
the sidewalk glittering outside of church,

or getting our cards back when Sunday is over,
the game my sisters and I loved to play,
its object to cheat and get caught, accuse
and roar with laughter. I like to think

there are rules in the Bible like that, God
shuffles the deck with great leaping arcs, deals in
the one standing on the edge sucking her lip.
Maybe we get aces slipped off the bottom,

and the game shifts so fast, everything's wild,
loser takes all. What was our mother thinking
when she put away those cards, took our matches
and pennies, called everything she didn't want us to be,

common? In her Bible with its dog-eared pages,
isn't it hustlers and cheats who fall on their knees?
I used to pray for another childhood, and here it is,
my son's, here's the dog I never had, a sweet one

we name *Stray* for the way she came to us,
loping out of nowhere, worm-ridden, mangy,
tearing sheets off the line, and every time my son
calls her in from the fields, we can almost hear

God calling the used, the thrown out, the scolded,
a child with her head down, hands twisted
around a wad of blue dress, who ought
to just hush now, who ought to be ashamed

for the way she slammed into those wet sheets
with her dirty hands, whooping it up, pretending
they were walls she could pass through—
but that is the past now, now she has to let go.

HOOD

I can still see the hand-painted signs
on ghetto fences: *Keep Out, Attack Dog,*
and just enough of them not bluffing
it must have given our gangster neighbor

the idea: his own loping Great Dane
one of those. So, paper bag over his head,
he jabbed a broomstick into the dog's chest
again and again, as if her whimpers enraged him,

and that combined dog-cry, man-howl
filled the block like thick industrial smoke.
In goes the meanness, *out* goes the baffled hurt
of her yelps, or so he must have reasoned.

But what's reason to a dog, who just likes
dirt cool on her belly, likes a tight squeeze
through the fence, the sudden fragrance
of a neighbor's garden? What is reason

to her unwary joy, who licked crumbs
off our fingers, followed mailmen and cops
down the block, racing ahead, trotting back
for a rub? He must have thought it out:

that broom, the bag hiding his face.
But when he lunged, putting his whole body
into each jab, did another argument take over:
blood smell, old rage, a cornered hood

turning on what he loves, or loving only
that turn, the snap of another's will?
I can still hear those bewildered yips,
as if the dog, trembling in her pen,

just couldn't get the next part
of the lesson we were hearing
all over the block: first hurt, then fear,
then the clenched heart's furious growl.

PINK SLIP

Twenty years I gripped your press,
yanked down as the belt rattled past.
You stamped my checks, the bank sent letters
saying what I owed on my house, my car,
my teeth. Now the expressway roars overhead,
and how can I argue back, when I can't

even get my car out of the tow lot?
Inside the gatekeeper's shed a TV surfs
out of control: soap commercial, canned laughter,
profile of Martin Luther King, skinny woman
stepping out of a fat woman's clothes—
as I would like to step out of this night

onto the last day of earth and accuse you
once again, only now with smoke and lights,
some kind of music to back me up:
how my kids are the same age as yours,
my kids, with too many teeth in their heads,
and one who still can't pronounce *thr*—.

All you did was check your watch,
all you did was back me to the door,
where outside they were hauling my car,
a pirate company, so not even the cops
could say where it is. Is this America?
I've seen countries on TV where the natives

give funny looks to the fat men they serve
drinks to on patios. "Bastard," would be
my translation. Or whatever the deaf woman
is banging onto the locked windows of cars
jammed at the on-ramp trying to leave the city.
You on your top floor look down, waiting

for the crowd to thin, you with those women
in high heels printing out memos that shut
down a whole plant. You're calm now.
But if just one loony on the picket line
decides to fling a bucket of paint,
if a pack of kids with bats comes hooting out

of a bar, you wouldn't have a clue.
One more John Doe in fancy clothes,
high-class words foaming on your lips,
but just as helpless, you bastard,
at the end of the world, if there is an end,
if people like me get to rise up and speak.

DOGS

What mongrel delight they took, crashing my backyard
parties, clattering teacups, trampling mud cakes.
I'd race up Grandmother's brick steps,
bang at her door, panicked by that hot breath
on my thighs, as if somewhere inside
I'd already been bitten—the way so many friends now
are remembering how their own fathers
nosed into their beds, snarled "Hush" so fiercely,
for years those daughters could not tell even themselves
where he put his hands, how he seared the body.
What is such a father, but a dog gone wild, snapping
its chain, obsessed with its own howling needs?
Once a friend's grandmother called her
a dog—however you say it in Yiddish—
for nuzzling in the soft lap of another woman.
"How's *The Dog?*" Grandma would shout every week
into the phone, meaning something more complicated
than I just yelled at my son—"Cut that out"—for tossing a ball
to his dog beside the Christmas tree, and yes—not the tree—
but everything else came down, broken cup, coffee
soaking the papers I graded. The dog just sat
by the tinselly branches staring, as if my scolding,
my son's scowl, our fury of mopping didn't exist.
It's a look I saw once on a man whose dog had bitten me
as I jogged past his drive, whose pug-faced mongrel
had sunk its teeth so deep into my leg I fainted.
With a sheet of questions from the clinic,
I drove back to that battered house and watched
as the man rose slowly, put down his coffee-can spittoon,
cracked the door and stared just past me. Gaunt, pale,
expressionless, "I got no dog," he said,
as if something fiercer than that
had sunk its teeth into him so deep his whole life
had drained out to ease the pain. My friend,
The Dog, was at a stoplight when her father
came rushing back from the darkness, flashing
his naked body through an open robe,
licking her taste off his lips. Amazing
how little rage she felt pulling off the road.
He was dead, having forced on her,

she said, the fact of her own
body, its hunger and juice, loyalty, shame.
"Emblem of faithfulness," we read last night
under museum glass: "found at the feet of women
engraved on medieval tombs." Can't you see it,
ear cocked for the slightest motion?
"Symbol of resurrection," it said—
as if who else would track us that far,
who else gladly sniff and lick
after we've been so drastically transformed?

MIDNIGHT FLOWERS

Pulped by flood waters, my favorite picture book
   is gone, the whole 1930s unreprinted story—
     elfin town sunk into cumulus dark
      by a sad boy-prince's deep sighs.

Something about townsfolk like parents
   clucking, *Come, cheer up*, as if the boy chose
     to grow listless and lose his appetite.
      Then something about bakers parading cakes,

one sailing a candle-lit boat through dark canals,
   plucking huge orange and blue flowers.
     Long after I could read, what I loved to read
      most were those bright quirky flowers,

each stalk shining its bold lurch of flashlight
   into the pitch-black field. And that's how
     it felt after the flood, staggering back
      from evacuation—an eye feast

of sun-stippled trees bursting with green,
   birds manic with the boom in nesting materials.
     Under their garish exuberant wings,
      we shoveled sludge, fridge insulation

bubbling out like pink chemical ooze,
   Janson's tweedy *History of Art*—reduced
     to gray fibrous scrim kids dry on old screens,
      making paper in school. For days

my picture book lingered on the sidewalk
   in bright stains, flame-yellow and flower-blue,
     a kind of Pollock design, object turning
      to energy, colored swirls mixed into

the concrete's nicks and trowel marks, loss
   just a change of form. What finally cheered
     the young prince—was it that cake mixed from
      midnight flowers, as if someone showed him

what can bloom in darkness, how night breaks
    from within, a cocoon cracking, light rushing
        like the river that swept between trees, over
            doorsills, sloshing against our walls.

All those feathered makers and doers,
    frantically yanking couch stuffing and scarves,
        snatching yarn still kinky as they trail it up
            to their crazy-quilted nests—let them.

And let the child have her sighs, her rivers
    of darkness, let her bob and tilt on those
        turbulent rills, drifting through night
            shiny as hard-pressed crayons. Let her stare

at flowers drawn as if each had its own klieg light,
    so years later when she closes her eyes
        she'll still find them—fluorescent, almost
            perfect replicas flooding the blackness.

BABYSITTING TO THELONIOUS MONK

My niece wants eggs, now, please, and I swirl
hot water around the poaching whites
so they won't fray into cloudy blurs.
She's centrifugal too, black in a family
of white, thick scowl the other kids love to tease.
So she spins in her own dark skin like the water
bucket she swings overhead to see

if the force is real. But her arm gets
tired and the pail dumps itself in
one plop on her head, a private cloud
always threatening to spill. Light tap on her crown
like pretend eggs running down, and she's off again,
eyes closed, slow, a tiny Thelonious Monk,
who also turned like this, on bandstands,

in lobbies—comforting himself or
keeping in the demons. Or maybe
it was his fine-tuned ears scanning for
a new sense in dissonance, the way a beat teases
itself, melody flits like a butterfly, settles,
takes off, no need to pin down. A grownup taste,
unlike this child who wants more, more, now,

little sister of something missing
from long ago. It's what she knows, racks
of candy, checkout line's hot gimme
and grab. I put on Monk to settle us down,
and she whistles back what she hears—his last recording
before the grim silence of crack-up, as if music
can outwit it just so long. She's fed,

but how can that be enough? Spinning
again, on the lawn, arms spread, she wraps
the neighborhood around her till she
is the core. Then gravity takes over, her engine
sputters, she's banking, ground coming up slanted
in her face. She's down, a green consultation
of maples swaying above her: Yes,

she'll live, she'll pop up, do it again,
fall dizzy, watching trees, lamp post, house
swirl a minute before they stiffen
to gridlock—same minute Monk expands, slows down to
one note at a time, picks up again like water
pooling in her small dark hands, spilling through fingers
till spilling, Child, is what it's about.

A KIND OF DARKNESS

Butterflies—those sailboats of the insect world,
serene among engine gunners, like our best thoughts
rising without fuel, free of ambition's guzzle.

But once, jogging an old farm road, I saw
a rabbit carcass swarmed by yellow wings
nibbling, sniffing, not budging when I stomped,

the way in some parts of town figures huddle
to pass a needle or pipe, so starved for it
not even flashing lights disperse their concentration.

Imagine—those frail Velcro mouths wolf-hungry,
flitting from death to death, the way I used to
fear my grandmother's wet kisses, pressed

from lip to lip, would spread old age.
She died, one whole side of her body purple
from the fall, a grimace stiffened on her face

the undertaker had to hammer out.
I can hardly stand the thought that her longed-for
afterlife wasn't all floating clouds and praise,

but a moment of throat-locked suffocation,
and then—Hieronymus Bosch! Maybe I didn't see
those bright petal-thin wings on the dead rabbit,

maybe the twist in my grandmother's face
was more like the sirening howl karate choppers
let out striking a pile of bricks—say the wall

between *this* world and *that*, as if heaven's
a realm so strange it's only entered by force.
The year we moved north to the city,

we asked our young daughter what she missed most,
and butterflies flew from her mouth—yellow,
orange, black and white, striped and plain, blue ones too.

Then a sigh, and *purple*, she cried, stomping off,
leaving us helpless against that mystic garden
forming in her mind, its tale of banishment and loss.

Maybe it wasn't for her we dug out the book
showing how purple exists—under crisp tissues,
in such frail powdery glitter, it's as if

the crushed wings of a real one had been reformed
on the page. Natural habitat: Cameroon, Brazil,
and that bright world always flickering at the edge

of sight, that iridescence sunlight makes
out of dust on wings, out of anything distant,
while *here* is a kind of darkness we tear at.

BETWEEN PICKETS

Remember the steep houses with picket fences,
the curls of chimney smoke we used to draw
in school, even kids who lived in beat-up trailers
heated by an open oven door—and how the sun
in those pictures grinned from a thin margin
of blue sky? That's what the inmates in my class

say they want: a past innocent of the bad ends
they've come to, or the long middle blurred
by alcohol and crystal meth, rage,
the constant figuring of odds. But faced
with Claudette's awful rhymes, her *arms*
& *charms*, I hound for details: broken cassette,

one shoe, black shawl spilling from the love car
that hit ice and rammed a tree. "The bottle
we drank was cold," I get her to write,
"your body lay submerged under ice . . ."
But I didn't ask for this: her father
sleeping with her till she was nine,

till her mother ripped the blankets off,
screaming *get out.* She isn't writing now,
but telling us he did nothing wrong, just
warmed her on cold nights, his hands making
her feel—I didn't ask for this—"electric
and dizzy in the dark, like liquor's buzz."

Such constant chatter. For weeks the others
have muttered *shut up,* but what to say now
to her father's boot jabs, her mother limp
on the floor—to this middle-aged woman
like a child drawing a skinny banner of sky
at the top of her page, claiming it's thanks

to her father, she's become so lovable?
Do we tell her the sky goes all the way down
into the thinnest spaces between pickets,
and there's a sadder word than *lovable* for her
constant crushes? Even if it doesn't look
like sky down here among the stylized tulips

at the bottom of the page, it is—because sky
is just air getting darker and colder as it
accumulates overhead. Isn't that what
they told us in school, we who never really drew
what we saw, but what we saw others drawing,
say, the girl with burn marks on her arms,

or the boy with so much on his mind, the teacher
could knock on his head, ask "anyone home?"
and even then he wouldn't answer. Sometimes
all those kids did in school was make elaborate
princess clothes, minutely detailed castles
with hidden escape routes. But even though

the inmates have seen how getaways fail,
no one stops Claudette from not driving again
that car "the f-ing judge" gave her 10 years for,
after the prosecutor rolled it—how many times—
down the ravine into a tree, making her lover's
dead eye stare up at her night after night.

All spring I've been pounding *detail, detail,*
as if that eye, the one shoe and pink receipt
from an oil change drifting on the icy pond
will add up to a better life. Her face is puffy
and lined, yet oddly girlish, scanning the room
like a kid afraid someone might grab her paper

and rip it up. Remember those curtains
we'd make with frontward and backward *R*'s,
the smoky script of little *e*'s we'd repeat
from chimney to sky—how we drew and drew,
and went on living in our real houses,
drifting somewhere slightly above our beds?

III

THE TINY GATE

The steady turning of pages, students murmuring
in the stacks, children in boots clomping the stairs
with armfuls of picture books, easy to read aloud—

but I remember a stammering child, an engine chug
that couldn't get started, who only spoke alone
under the blankets, or along the riverbank practicing

plosives, fricatives. She'd poke the shallows with a stick,
murmuring stories from an overdue book of *Saints*
Every Child Should Know: Joan's one phobia, fire,

how they broke chair legs, bed posts, brush wood,
raised her higher on the stake. They twisted oily rags
around a split branch. The girl dog-eared that page,

threw rocks in the water. Joan begged,
she writhed and shrieked as flames caught her hem,
then just when she thought she'd burst, the book said

the voices which had left her flew back. A whole
volume of this, each story a roller coaster ratcheting up
its steep laborious crank on flimsy scaffolding—

then lights! voices! wings!—a plunge into fluency,
the dream of a hesitant child. What she couldn't say
bunched up like paper and twigs snagged in the reeds.

Weeks late with the book, its spine cracked, clueless
how to answer the librarian's wagging finger—
"What have you done?"—stammering, stammering,

her mouth was a tiny gate. To pass through, the words
broke themselves again and again, so even now I feel
the weight of that child, wishing for the drunk's smooth tongue

at the front desk, demanding yesterday's paper.
And when he kneels down to beg, it's the soldier painted
in my old book, dropped to his knees, finding Joan's heart

still beating in the ashes, the ecstasy I never had:
this fellow in frayed tweed, enjoying every second of his plea,
of the librarian flapping her arms, crying "Out! Out!"

All those years of logjam, afternoons leaning over the bank,
wishing I could just give myself to that river—and now I see
the river was giving itself to me.

FINE ARTS

Riding a backpack through the museum, my son
would cry up the scale from suggestion to howl—
his first staccato sentence: *down, out, home, now.*
Was it that gallery of stern grandparents he couldn't
grin into sweet babblers? We'd hardly get

past them to Degas or Toulouse-Lautrec,
without a guard ushering us out. Never made it
to mummies, stiff as a game of statues
gone horribly wrong, without the bum's rush
to the lawn, where my boy happily waddled up

to cigarette butts and crumpled wrappers,
chased pigeons into flight, or tried to catch light
playing through leaves. Light in long shafts,
or high noon's neon—isn't that what painters love?
Sometimes after a snack, we'd try again,

rushing past ballerinas in pink, slumped on break
or stretching at the bar, torch singers in fishnet,
one calf exposed, so you can almost hear
a man's whiskey laugh, music pulsing the floor.
Then *out, now, down, home* would rise again,

and like art thieves, we'd duck the guards,
slipping into a crowd, past a tour guide's phrase,
marvelous instant. We'd snatch what we could
and make off—enough to see trolley tracks gleam,
or make a lone pigeon seem Picasso's invention.

And a whole flock? My boy would crane
to follow their swoop and rush till he toppled over,
learning the world's worth falling for,
not a bad place. On the steps there'd be
bigger boys with free passes scanning

the crowd for fake parents to shuffle them in,
as if art's guardians didn't trust them alone
in the basement Egyptian rooms, art's guardians
intent on making sure something that's outlived
almost unscathed, Aristotle, Suleiman,

53

Einstein, will outlive these boys as well.
Such an old debate: those who long to finger
mummy rags, or after the day at school want
to pencil, "Sue was here" on anything in sight—
versus—the guards with their "Mustn't disturb,"

as if they never saw how light in one mood
paints us gold and in the next just wants to
obliterate. What's a mother to do
but tell her son, if he wants *home*, it's his,
and if some spendthrift years lead through *down*

& *out*, through whiskey rush and throaty song?
Well, she'll tell herself that's not the end
of anything—after this *now*, there's another,
another marvelous instant, we're far
from closing, far from whatever that means.

VALENTINES

Why not fill the day with machines—Eddie
drilling holes through the house, burrowing in
like an electric woodpecker, littering
the ground with bits of chewed up egg cartons
and wooden plugs; Steve at SpeeDee Lube
draining transmission fluid, replacing

a halogen light; the girl up front—
that's what she called herself on the phone
while I read *Newsweek* on "Talking to God."
A woman on the other end must have been
holding jumper cables in each hand. "Which is
which," she must have asked, and the cashier said,

"I don't know, I'm just a girl myself"—
though one with two dozen roses on her desk,
two cards and vases, two men wanting
to hook up, and she'll have to decide.
Insulation rumbles into the wall
like a car riding on a flat tire.

The doorbell gets two quick rings, and now,
our daughter has six roses and a big heart—
not a thick muscular pump, but that bright
romantic shape we've abstracted from need,
the way the greasy *Newsweek* said ideal
prayer moves from wanting things to gratitude.

I'd like to know where it comes from, that shape
we call a heart. Was it, as you read last night,
St. Valentine in prison pricking holes
in violet leaves, slipping them through bars
to passersby: "I'm well," "God's good," "Take heart"—
proto-messages for the pale sugary

candies stamped *Hey Girl* and *Oh, Babe,*
that our daughter separates into piles
so her boyfriend gets all *Kiss Me* and *Yes?*
We eat what's left, those *Not Nows* and *Back Offs*
melting in our sluggish parental blood.
This is the day in medieval times

they thought birds found their mates,
day of fanfare and flutter, day of bright
rise and dip through air, making bird love,
however they do it, conceiving those
fragile worlds they'll hover and tend
till the hunger inside breaks out, noisy

and possessive as a jilted guy
with a huge florist bill, but singing
about it so well we can't believe
the subtext hasn't moved from greed to God,
birds crooning their bright jazz fugues,
a gratitude of cracked seed husks on the ground.

All day at the feeder purple finches
gathered then flitted off when Eddie cranked
the ladder. One left, came back, shook
her tail like a show girl in high heels
and some outlandish garb with plumes,
gave another turn, an extra wiggle

before she was gone, just a bird again,
a girl with mouths to feed, aching feet,
dead battery, whole lot of uncertainty
in each hand, and I'd like to believe, Love,
a patron saint telling her, "Big deal, Honey.
So what if you get them wrong?"

AUTOBIOGRAPHY IN THIRD PERSON

Though she was born late in their lives,
she was not the error her parents feared,
her father's nightmare that she'd emerge
quoting Nietzsche, her mother's worry
that she'd not take to quoting at all.

Still, who doesn't have pages they'd like to
rip from the calendar? For her it is March,
month of freezing rain and downed wires,
Irish moon rising, first ruddy, then blanched,
like her father's bones glaring in the ground.

Deceased, her mother taught her to say,
not *dead*. *Dead* was crude, bones growing
rancid. *Deceased* was a piece of paper,
officially stamped, or a tiny blue spiral
notebook in which she was to record

her moods, then throw them away.
Oh moon heat river paradox running
siren blue uphill as exhaust flakes
rustle down—that was found years later
nearly illegible on her bedside table,

tucked in the marbled notebook where
she re-examines the question obsessing her
juvenilia: Does air, like fog, obscure
the view, blurring color, so one must
choose between clarity and breath?

Does survival depend on distortion,
so the greatest toxin of all is truth?
In that same notebook, recorded
from the last page forward, are dreams.
First, the one where she tries to prod

from the earth a giant stone, the way a pack
of hoodlums would rock a car. But it is huge
and barely grunts, a rancid, pissed off Buddha
bent on breaking impossible desire.
Next, the Mexican beauty parlor, chickens

out front deconstructing the ground. She asks
for color and curls, but the old woman says,
"No, too much—have to choose, choose."
A man with no teeth and a portable phone
is trading in futures. The word *choose*

in different scripts curls through the margins.
Clipped to that page, the draft of a letter,
dated the fourth of March, asks what if
the premise is false, the whole notion of some
reign of error: "Perhaps, Doctor, it's just

a lack of coolant in my veins. What's so sick
about wanting a ghost that doesn't rise
to the surface, mouth some inaudible code,
then slip out of the hands like soap, like
lavender-scented diaphanous soap?"

MONKEY HOUSE

Such a howl went up when I walked in,
big lippy kisses and hoots so loud
I couldn't help but turn. Then as I stepped away,
wails, head clobbering. We did that
over and over—kiss-kiss and head-conk—
barely noticing the crowd. I never saw
such hairy grief, big knuckled loneliness
scraping the floor. *Closer,*

he motioned, *closer*— just the opposite
of my humanoid family, those dreary
worriers, who'd like to zap out of the genes
any feeling that can't sit like a lady,
keep its elbows off the table. Stuff it back in
and stay calm, they insist, or we'll all be
hurled down dark eons, back into furry faces
and curled toes, shitting on floors.

I started pacing in front of the cage,
a one-person house of hysterics. Other visitors
carefully tip-toed around. The chimp lay
on his back, picked his toes, pursed his great
flexible lips, and I was about to say: my people
didn't use words, they did it with eyebrows, tiny
sucked-in breaths, obsessive as painting on grains
of rice with brushes made from one split hair—

but then I looked up at his body, its big
furry smarts, the way whatever he did
he did completely, reaching an arm behind
his head to get to his chin, fizzing his face up
like a seltzer bottle. "You feel what you feel,"
I said, and he rolled his eyes, looking
everywhere but at me, as if to say,
"Interview over. You got what you came for."

And suddenly he was limp, slumped over,
as though a grief too big to thump or shriek
had dropped down on his shoulders, a sorrow
cut deep over what's become of his kind.

I put my palms to the glass where his had been,
as if I could feel the rough pads of his fingers,
a trace of that heat meant for a whole jungle
now crammed into one very small house.

HALFWAY

Tolstoy or Camus or something denser,
I don't care, she was always reading:
in elevators, or waiting for a ride
while the rest of us chatted—students hired
to set up a halfway house for mental patients:
in the car at night, book tilted to catch
the street light, at bus stops, in restaurants,
her hair a fine silk veil straining out
the contamination of our eyes.
Few people in my life I've wanted to smack,
but she's one. I am another—left over
from the days of my childhood stammer,
seeing through someone else's eyes
as I butted my head, how they wanted
to fast forward, to yank or shove me
over the block. Little good it does.
The patients were wiser, knowing who to rush,
who to skirt at meetings where they planned
new lives. They were breaking out from walls,
from shuffle and haze, from head banging
or birdlike fright. And suburban smugness
was breaking out, town after town: zoning
refused. Asked where they thought the patients
came from, whose fathers, sisters, aunts—
a town's lawyers and housewives would erupt
as if they were the nuts, splitting off
from all that wasn't manicured, zipped and sure.
While the rest of us took that furious heat,
our reader sat in each town hall's back row,
cool head bowed, exclusion personified,
or—we joked—on *books* instead of thorazine.
Couldn't she see that the more she read,
the more our anger rose, as if her attempts to avoid
only upped the pressure in some tank of ink,
its thick unrefined reserves swelling toward
barely articulate shrieks? I was there
only by marriage, a team member's new wife,
learning my own liberation through lips,
direct address set free of speech, mouths
suddenly fluent with love. So I hate to say

how good it felt snatching the book from her lap,
watching her shrink into crimped eyes, hands
on her ears so she could hear the blood inside
drumming *run, run,* as we circled her chair.
Who couldn't feel their innocence crumble
that summer? Who didn't stand in the rubble
of their own good selves, having to choose
whether to rebuild the walls or step away
suddenly exposed and raw? The halfway house
ended up on hospital grounds instead
of those unwilling towns the patients came from.
They gave up a lot to be set free—
the private comforts of rocking, sucking
on thumbs, other things I don't need to name
because you know them. And you know too
when you see someone on your block searching
for cans as if it's hard work, it *is* hard work,
being in this world, remembering
your radio is not God, eyes are not
laser swords, and if the water racing down
the bus stop's scuffed Plexiglas windbreak
speaks to you, what it will say is *rain,*
clamorous *rain,* impossible to control.

FALLING

When the house began to tip, I stepped back,
trying to save it, or me, or both. Was it wrong
to climb the ladder rungs nailed to the trunk,
to squeeze through porthole plank rot?
Should I have stayed on the ground, not leaned
toward the river's meandering flash
I wouldn't have known was there?
How could I have known that brief leafy
diversion would fling me out, door
after random extravagant door,
thick shingles of green tearing, green
hinges snapping, broken off from the rest
and frozen in my mind, so again and again,
for months, in traffic or on the edge of sleep,
I am let loose and flailing, finding myself
on the verge, almost bird in the brief
clumsy flight a fall is before landing.
I have seen little birds drop straight down
as if their wings were glued, and I have seen
old movies where they play a jump backward
to trick us, and succeed, because who doesn't
want to soar, to rise in reverse up
ladders of air? But to get there
we'd have to enter the teetering house,
let go when we want most to hold on,
want *up* so badly we refuse the *down*
it's made of, the whole clattering drop.
And what of the other world, invisible
to this, glimpsed a split second in the river's
quicksilver through branches, a flicker
on the edge of thought, and gone?
Could I have flown there and plucked a twig,
could I have healed the tumbling house?
The man who loves me and watched
from outside, says he still trembles seeing me
draped rag-limp over the wrecked sill,
says he thought he was watching my death,
and don't call it by another name.
But could death really be that green,

the river's flickering gleam
and those little birds in their plain brown wrappers
who just before crash flash their wings,
vanishing through a hedge of light?

FOUR CROWS AT DUSK

Perched on a steep slate roof: the first—
God knows what it wants, all squawk,
like it's deaf and has to shout remarks
about a blonde in short-shorts, a couple
kissing in the street, motorcycle revving.

The second's got an itch it can't quite reach,
so it bites and yanks, wing stuck out
like a banging shutter. Number three
doesn't like its position, hops to the end—
no better. Hops back, shimmies its tail,

drops something. More glob than bird,
the squawker's quiet now, as if it ran down
mid-sentence, having made the same point
thirty years. The preener is calm too, spent,
like a sob subsiding. The last one sits

and stares, turns its head now and then,
or you wouldn't even know it was a bird.
You'd think maybe a tired bowtie,
or a black, half-wilted rose. Not one
of four crows on a steep church roof

starting to crumble—till it flies off,
leaving three, and a little girl on a big-wheel
not answering when her mother hollers
from an upstairs window, "You're gonna
get it, I'm gonna whip your butt": three

& the other on a wire now, call and response
blacking out those threats, so the child keeps
clattering down the block. Bad girl birds,
raspy voices in your head—"Way to go, kid.
Hot damn"—as if every gripe, every flash

of rage you thought you'd regret takes the stage
now in a gospel quartet, the four black-robed
survival sisters—half-hoarse soloist at the mike,
wailing her been-through-the-fire, got-burnt,
but-it-ain't-over-yet-honey good news.

SPARROWS

My neighbor's tree was simmering,
a spruce bubbling over with chirps, louder
than the city garbage truck idling at the curb,

louder than my own mind saying, "Those guys
think you're nuts." Or my other mind asking,
"how can you ignore the music boiling in this tree?"

So I shook the long green sleeves of its branches,
hoping to see that song's belly and wings,
its little wiry feet, to flush out those notes

jumping through dense staves, those quick
flickering heartbeats pulsing from limb to limb.
I know people get struck for this, some wisdom

can cost fingers or eyes. We get sent back
to some place very old, where things are only
half-converted, earth clods still clinging to roots,

mouths clotted with beard hair and consonants.
There, a tree is more than a tree, still part-god,
knowing things, screeching when cut.

Even the cross weeps then, a bitter speech,
baring its soul. The truck idled, clusters
of junior high kids made an elaborate ritual

out of snapping Zippos, taking long drags,
but there was a door I could close on that,
I could squeeze between branches, press against

the trunk, letting those birds bite—that's what
I imagined—the birds yanking my hair, the mouths
that made the music, making music out of me.

But I was afraid of that wanting, afraid
of the way wanting I don't even know I have
sometimes leaks from my face, so a stranger

out of nowhere will offer a smoke.
Is it just a matter of degrees between him & me,
and the crazy woman who walks our streets,

gesturing wildly—her arms all leathery tendon,
as if the desire she's vagrant with is flight,
her body a semaphore, coaxing down spirits

or fending them off. The birds were quiet now.
I wanted to chase them out, to see how many
and what kind. I wanted their music all over me

like mosquito bites, swarming the way in sci fi movies
a sound can make you writhe on the ground.
Perhaps they'd think I *was* the tree and get impatient

with hiding—small grayish birds, dozens of them,
sparrows maybe. I wanted to hold one in my hand,
its fierce panic fluttering through me.

Isn't the afterlife full of creatures who think like this—
that fox, for instance, who jumps and jumps at grapes
dangling just out of reach. He'd probably like

a fat little sparrow, then a rain puddle to rinse
the feathers from his mouth. And what if God
is listening right now? What if God is thinking,

"give her what she wants," so suddenly
my arms are green, my legs hard and shaggy,
impossible to move. When does it go too far?

3

Music and desire, that spontaneous combustion—
I half-remember a man crouched in a belfry
and ringers tugging the heavy ropes:

down they pull, and up they're lifted, as one
after another, huge bell after lumbering bell
swings and tolls, and the poor fellow grips his head,

collapses, blood trickling from his ears ... One side
of my mind takes this as proof: "salt, stone,
straitjacket for you." But the other also threatens:

"you already are stone, if you don't get close
to that music." So it goes, the yammering debate.
Meanwhile, the tree frays and sparks like hot wires,

sound spatters and pours. Not ache or longing—
that's us, pulling the limbs, hoping to be lifted.
For them it must be all arrival, pure *here here*

now here, a flock of tongueless flames splashing out
like sterno, and nothing's charred. The spruce
is young, but still it's been standing a long time

with nothing but the usual wind, rain, sun, until now.
Nothing? Usual? That was my first mistake.
And I didn't know how long it could take,

standing, pricked by those branches, trying to see
the music, or the plump purple light of grapes,
or the sad eyes of the crazy woman the junior high kids

love to tease—to see and not grasp, but be grasped,
to stand here whether anything flickers, bursts
lit and singing from the tree, or nothing does.

DON'T EXPLAIN

I just wanted to tell what I saw—
a brown river, the Raritan, sprinkled
with loosestrife petals, two cassette tapes
dangling from a high bridge, rippled and looping
like kite strings in the wind—but questions came in:
what was the music, snagged on dirty heads,
tossed from a car speeding over the bridge?
And since my father went to school here, could he
have stood at this culvert, stripping petals
into the river? Back then, did flocks of geese
trample the bank down to stark red clay?
Over the phone, Mother says, *Oh sure, sure,*
to the brown water, to loosestrife and geese,
oh sure, the way she'd answer years ago
when I asked, Did they have cars back then? trains?
records? Later there were questions I didn't ask,
darker things—Did you know the same years you were
in school, Billie Holiday was scrubbing floors
in a whorehouse, playing Louis Armstrong
on an old Victrola? That would make Mother wince.
Ditto, if I asked, Were you ever so mad
you could've ripped out your favorite tape
and hurled it, so mad you half understand
the video—Woodstock redux—*Nine Inch Nails*
out-Hendrixing Hendrix, destroying something
they love *and* hate, yanking the keyboard
from its sockets, smashing guitar on amp,
again and again till only the drummer's
left, ducking hurled mikes—God.
I wanted to say wind unraveled those tapes
like an aria too beautiful to be heard,
so we have to imagine the song we'd play
till it wore out, then carry on inside us, wound
on spools of feeling that could spin it to mind any time.
That's what my dead father was to me—on a reel
for my comfort, better than life, till the night
I sat up reading in his own hand, letters
full of slurs, doors he wanted shut against
just about everyone. All night as I read,
my old tape slowed to the indecipherable

rumble of dead batteries and I ripped it out.
Though maybe it snagged on some undergirding
in my mind and still hangs, now limp, now billowing,
inaudible aftermath of rage, small lull
in the music, which lasts a while till something
shakes it up—the way two joggers saw me
on the culvert and just had to shout, *Don't jump,
ha ha.* Balance almost begs for that,
as if whatever made my father so intent
on closing doors, is what makes us now want
to hear the voices that were shut out, want
to rewind and play again the band hurling
instruments and mikes, dumping water buckets
on the crowd dancing in a lumbered frenzy,
young kids lost in the song, whipping their heads
so wet hair stings their faces, feeling part of
the muddy ground, not caring where the crowd
carries them as long as they're moving. And now
the static and screech—is this my father's lost voice
singing inside me, *The world's going down. And down*—
me singing back—*in order to rise?* Down
to where no one's shut out, down to the riverbank's
bare red clay, down to a voice like Holiday's,
that even on a bad tape made from old records,
sends her losses straight to the marrow—*Don't Explain,
Strange Fruit*—voice totally shot by the end,
as if the life couldn't be kept out,
the music couldn't keep itself from breaking.

REDBUD

I had to step outside, having just finished
the letters of Keats, who for all his talk of easeful death,
told his friend Brown he wanted to live, wanted his *feeling
for light and shade*, his memories of walking with her—
everything reminds him. *Oh God! God! God!*—
he was barely able to write it, *I should have had her
when I was in health*. Does that mean what it sounds like to us?
Window light and leaf shade on the porch. Next door,
people slipping into their coats, leaving a party. *See ya, Take it easy.*
Hard to believe just last week, I looked up to see a blue truck
crest the hill, flying it seemed, and the driver's surprised eyes
as he fishtailed into me. Barely time to ask, *Am I going to die?*
But nobody did, so can I say it was worth it? say that *beauty*
totaled my car—the stand of redbuds I'd gone to see, purple blossoms
on rain-slick limbs, stark as petals on a painted scroll blooming
above waterfalls, above tiny figures on a foot bridge crossing
a steep gorge. There we were, waiting for a trooper in that fellow's cab,
and it seemed he had to tell how he got caught cheating his boss
at the stables, how he was planning to leave a whole mess
of bad credit, racing stubs, a woman who finally said, *Get out.*
Beauty must have been a kind of charm he knew how to use,
aqua eyes, easy smile, the way he could tell his scam and still run it,
share a thermos, ask ideas for his new name. All around us, those redbuds
so stunning I can't remember now if he drugged a horse,
or fixed a race, dealt off the bottom with his fine jittery hands.
I had Keats in my pocket, himself worried about money,
walking through Scotland to see its waterfalls, astonished
by what he hadn't imagined, the subtleties of tone—moss, rock-weed—
I live in the eye he says to his brother. But they're gone—
Keats, Fanny, Tom, everyone he wrote those exuberant letters to.
What good is *beauty*? Still I saw it, those redbuds, like the moment
making love, into the rush of it, when you think, *I could die now.*
After which—the truck, that fellow telling the trooper flat out
he was doing 50 in a 25, as if beauty has to press its luck,
which the insurance company said had run out:
we'll get him, don't you worry. I don't.
Because he's gone, among the tossing heads of horses,
their nervous sidesteps—gone, without a name,
like those tiny figures dissolving in paint. Imagine,

standing over a gorge where a waterfall plummets—lost,
not so much in thought as its graceful absence, so lost
there is nothing else to want from the world. The *world.*
How beautiful the word sounds. *Whorled.* Purple blossoms
on rain-black trees. The enormous eyes of horses. Rock-weed, slate.
The world loving us, who probably have never loved enough,
never dared let ourselves go that far into its beauty.